GOLF ADDICTS TO THE FORE!

BY THE SAME AUTHOR

Confessions of a Golf Addict	Museum Press
More Confessions of a Golf Addict	Museum Press
Golfers' Treasury	George Newnes
The *Full* Confessions of a Golf Addict	Pelham Books Ltd.
Golf Addict Omnibus	Country Life Books
Golf Addict Goes East	Country Life Books
Golf Addict Among the Scots	Country Life Books
Golf Addict Invades Wales	Pelham Books Ltd.
Golf Addict in Gaucho Land	Pelham Books Ltd.
How to be a Golf Addict	Pelham Books Ltd.
Just a Friendly . . .	Leslie Frewin
Believe It or Not - That's Golf	Wm. Luscombe Ltd.

GOLF ADDICTS
To The Fore!

CARTOONS BY

George Houghton

GORDON WRIGHT PUBLISHING
25 MAYFIELD ROAD, EDINBURGH EH9 2NQ
SCOTLAND

British Library Cataloguing in Publication Data

Houghton, George
   Golf addicts to the fore!
   1. English wit and humour, Pictorial
   1. Title
   741.5'942   NC1479

ISBN 0-903065-53-3

Typeset by Gordon Wright.
Printed by Billing and Sons Ltd. Worcester.

Fore-Word

Eureka! I am about to explain golf humour.

If you believe *that* you'll believe anything. No one can explain golf humour. The subject is much too subtle.

Humour in golf is an imponderable. Magical, completely essential to the game, yet hated by the sourpusses who learn the rules, wag a stick at the ball and imagine they are playing golf. I defy anyone to explain what it is all about.

Some quite nice people honestly believe that an amalgam of laughter and golf does not exist. They consider that a laugh by someone who has just played a bad shot is as inappropriate as a cheer accompanying the death rattle.

The majority of participants, I am pleased to say, enjoy the warm fun contained in every golf gesture and comment appertaining to the game. Those are my customers. They send me detailed accounts of how they have made damned fools of themselves. They want nothing more than that I draw their foolishness and record their golf comments for posterity.

As one would expect, golf is full of extraordinary complexities. The novelist Berta Ruck told me that she clearly remembered her young cousin Bernard Darwin who was never really happy 'unless he was slashing about in the deep rough on the Aberdovey golf links'. Imagine that, if you can, the boy who was to become the high priest of golf expressing joy with a niblick!

David Lloyd George, who was 12-handicap at Walton Heath and, even at the height of the Kaiser war, played with the great James Braid every Wednesday afternoon, said, 'Golf is the only game known to man where the worst player gets the best of it.

More exercise, and more enjoyment. The good player worries over mistakes, whereas the poor player makes too many mistakes to worry.'

Harold Macmillan was once chased off the Nairn links by suffragettes and only worried because he suspected they had not paid their green fees!

Some say there is no humour in golf. Others maintain that every aspect of the game produces a smile of unadulterated joy. Lee Trevino says he plays best when his gags succeed with the crowd. Bob Hope once offered to lend him a gag-writer; this was refused by Lee who said, 'If I can't find enough in this game to make people laugh I shouldn't be playing.'

Golf is the right environment for jokes. 'Not a bad pair of whippy shafts,' said the cartoonist H.H.Harris, pointing at his pencil-thin legs exposed in his new pair of check plus-fours. That was on the first tee at Worthing and Harris was enjoying a laugh against himself. We all wished we had made the remark, even if it meant buying new plus-fours to get the attention.

The fantastic truth must be acknowledged. *Golfers like being laughed at.* Despite years of psychic probing no one has yet discovered why golfers revel in personal ridicule, while other sportsmen cringe with embarrassment. Let's face it, we are a race apart.

In this collection of cartoons, I derive my humour from wry comment or incidents which could only be seen on a golf course. Other than to dyed-in-the-wool players, my golf cartoons are meaningless. I try not to be frivolous because someone could always say, 'You are laughing at something I love.'

Nothing is so wounding as an opponent's lack of interest when you attack the ball. One feels that half the venom that goes into a really well-smacked drive should rightly have descended on the opponent's pate. Yet golf is not a vicious game. Discord seldom occurs. Ours is a gentle pursuit, played by nice people, and I sincerely hope that some of the sweetness seeps through into these cartoons.

The drawings come from some of my previous publications and my Golf Addict Calendars which made an initial, somewhat hesitant bow in 1952. Since then they have never missed a year, and it has been possible to make a selection from more than eight hundred cartoons.

Over the years I have learned a thing or two. For example, it is unwise to draw people in easily recognisable clothes. Fashions change and when the American folk hero Davy Crockett was popular enough for youngsters to wear furry hats with tails, it occurred to me that it would make a funny picture if I had a golfer wearing a Davy Crockett hat and saying, 'It might help with my putting.' Unfortunately, because the cartoons are done well ahead, by the time this one appeared in print, David Crockett and his hat were as dead as a dodo.

My old golfing pal Ted Ray used to say that folk will laugh at anything if the circumstances and build-up are right. Ted proved this. On the golf course he used to wave a cheery 'What ho' to any greens-keeper we passed. His simple greeting invariably brought a good laugh because folk thought that anything Ted Ray said must be funny.

Golf creates the happy mood and everything is great fun.

George Houghton
Dorset 1985.

'AM I RIGHT IN ASSUMING THAT YOU'VE WON
FIFTY PENCE ?'

'LOOK AT IT THIS WAY, SIR, IS TWO HUNDRED
POUNDS TOO MUCH TO INVEST IN A FUTURE
OPEN CHAMPION?'

'MORNING GIRLS - REPLACED THE FLAGS ?'

' - BUT YOU JUST TRY AND GET HIM TO PADDLE
WITH THE CHILDREN . . . !

'I THINK I'D BETTER STAY AT HOME TODAY, SIR...
AS YOU CAN HEAR, I'VE ALMOST LOST MY VOICE.'

'I TOLD YOU NOT TO BRING REPAINTS!'

'I SHOUTED FORE!'

'BUT SUPPOSING ONE HAS SWALLOWED IT ?'

'DON'T LET IT PUT YOU OFF, BUT MILLIONS OF
TELEVIEWERS ARE WATCHING THAT PUTT!'

'DON'T FORGET, THERE'S A PENALTY FOR
GROUNDING YOUR CLUB IN A BUNKER!'

'YOU'D NEVER SUSPECT THAT OUR ROSES ARE
COVERED WITH BLACK SPOT!'

'UGH - IT'S GOING TO BE ONE OF THOSE DAYS!'

'ALLOWING ME PARS ON THE FOUR HOLES
WHERE I THREE-PUTTED AND FORGETTING ALL
THAT NONSENSE AT THE THIRD AND EIGHTH . . .
I'VE REALLY HAD AN EXCELLENT ROUND!'

'PAH! NEW-FANGLED IDEAS! - I PREFER THE OLD WAY.'

'COME ON CHAPS, IT'S CLEARING.'

'HE SAYS THERE'S NOTHING WRONG WITH HIM
THAT EIGHTEEN HOLES WOULDN'T CURE.'

'I TOLD HIM NOT TO FEED THEM!'

'THEN, BELIEVE IT OR NOT, I MISSED MY PUTT!'

'IT'S THE ONLY WAY I CAN GET HIM TO DO
THE WEEDING.'

'MY IDEA IS TO ASK THE MEMBERS TO RALLY
ROUND AND LEVEL OFF THAT HILL.'

'AREN'T WE LUCKY! THE SOLICITOR WROTE TO
SAY BILL'S UNCLE LEFT US SOMETHING!'

'WILL HE BE LIVID IF I OFFER HIM A TIP ?'

'JUST HOW I LIKE IT - NO CROWDS ON THE
FIRST TEE.'

'FORBES BAGGED THAT WITH A BRASSIE SHOT!'

'I LET THE GOLFERS HAVE THIS LAND, BUT THEY
DON'T FERTILISE IT LIKE THE SHEEP.'

'... AND WHAT OTHER MAN LETS HIS WIFE COME
TO GOLF WITH HIM ?'

**WE'RE NOT DOING TOO BADLY - THERE'S THE
CLUBHOUSE!'**

'... AND WE DIDN'T COME TO PARIS TO WONDER
WHETHER YOU COULD CLEAR THE ARC DE
TRIOMPHE WITH AN EIGHT IRON SHOT!'

'YOU CONCENTRATE ON HOPING BOB FLUFFS HIS
DRIVES AND I'LL WORK ON JACK'S PUTTING.'

'YOU SHOULD HAVE SEEN THE ONE I HOLED AT
THE FIFTEENTH!'

'LET ME PUT IT THIS WAY, IF YOU WERE A GOLFER
I'D SAY YOU WERE DORMY FOUR DOWN.'

'DOCTOR SAYS I'M NOT BEING FAIR TO YOU IF I
DON'T TAKE EXERCISE.'

'DON'T JUST STAND THERE! - FIND OUT IF THIS
DITCH IS OUT OF BOUNDS.'

'MUST I BE INTRODUCED BY A MEMBER ?'

'SOMETIMES IT FRIGHTENS ME TO SEE HOW LIKE
HIS FATHER HE GETS . . .'

'HE MISSES IT.'

'WE CALL THIS HOLE "PLUNGING NECKLINE".'

'IT HASN'T QUITE STOPPED, OLD MAN.'

'NOW, THIS IS THE POSITION I WANT YOU TO GET –
BUT YOU MUST BE COMPLETELY RELAXED . . .'

'DOWN, RUFUS, I'VE TRIED ALL THAT, - HE WONT
TAKE EITHER OF US.'

'THERE'S NO NEED TO EXAGGERATE!'

'CAN YOU MANAGE A LITTLE SMILE ?'

'THERE'S A WAITING LIST - WHAT'S YOUR
HANDICAP ?'

'THERE GOES THE SKIPPER! - HE'LL WASH, GET CHANGED, HAVE A DRINK IN THE BAR, THEN HE'LL COME IN HERE AND GET SERVED BEFORE WE DO!'

'I THINK WE CAN ASSUME THAT THE SCOTTISH
TEAM HAVE WON THE FOURSOMES!'

'IT'S FRED - HE WANTS ME TO GIVE HIM A RIDE IN
OUR NEW CAR.'

'WE'LL LAUGH OUR HEADS OFF ABOUT THIS
TOMORROW.'

'IS THERE ANYTHING IN THE WORLD SO
WONDERFUL AS YOUR BEAUTIFUL SMILE - AND A
BIRDIE AT THE EIGHTEENTH . . . ?'

'THIS WASN'T WHAT I HAD IN MIND WHEN I
ASKED YOU TO TAKE ME FOR A DRIVE.'

'YOU GET ALL THE INTERESTING SHOTS!'

'THERE GOES ANOTHER SATISFIED CUSTOMER.'

'YOU CAN GO NOW - THERE'S NO-ONE IN THE BUNKER!'

'NO, IT ISN'T A MACHINE GUN!'

'DADDY'S WINNING - I KNOW THAT SMIRK.'

'OF COURSE, THIS WAS THE HIGHLIGHT OF THE
HOLIDAY.'

'HARRY VARDON DIDN'T HAVE THIS TO PUT UP
WITH!'

'WE MUST TRY TO CHANNEL THOSE FEELINGS OF
VICIOUSNESS INTO A VIABLE GOLF SWING.'

'ANY USE ME SUGGESTING THAT WE CHUCK IT ?'

'DAD, CAN I BORROW A COUPLE OF DECENT GOLF
BALLS - AND YOUR HOLE-IN-ONE TIE ?'

'I CAN'T INTERRUPT - THE CHAIRMAN IS
SUBMITTING A PROGRESS REPORT.'

'FRED'S HAD TOO MUCH PORT - THAT'S HIS
THIRD PAR!'

'GLADYS, CAN YOU HEAR ME ? I'VE QUALIFIED!'

'ARE YOU THE CHAP I WAS TELLING ABOUT MY
WHIPPY-SHAFTED DRIVER ?'

'IT'S A FEATURE OF THE COURSE - THEY TAKE AN
INTELLIGENT INTEREST.'

'EYE ON THE BALL, ALEC.'

'WHEN HE'S PUTTING I HAVE TO STAND BACK SO THAT THE SOUND OF MY BREATHING DOESN'T PUT HIM OFF - YET WHEN I ASK HIM TO HELP WITH THE WASHING-UP ...HE DOESN'T HEAR ME UNTIL I YELL LIKE MAD!'

'GUESS WHAT - I'M GOING TO LOWER YOUR
HANDICAP!'

'I SOMETIMES WONDER IF WE'VE GOT THE RIGHT
MAN AT THE HELM . . .'

'DO WE RUN OFF WITH IT ? - OR KICK IT IN AND
MAKE HIM BUY DRINKS ALL ROUND ?'

'ISN'T IT WONDERFUL - NO BUNKERS!'

'WE PLAY THE THREE HOLES SIX TIMES.'

'IT'S MY WIFE'S WAY OF SAYING I SHOULD BE
WORKING IN THE GARDEN!'

'STOP! - NOW WHAT WAS THE FIRST THING I TOLD
YOU ABOUT GOLF ?'

'HEAVENS! DOES IT EVER RAIN THAT HARD ?'

'THE WEAKNESS IN YOUR PUTTING IS
FUNDAMENTAL - YOU CAN'T AIM!'

' OF COURSE I'M PLEASED - BUT IS ALL SQUARE
WITH ONE TO PLAY THE TIME TO TELL ME THAT
YOU'RE GOING TO HAVE A BABY ?'

'I DON'T THINK THAT'S FUNNY!'

'I MAINTAIN THAT HAPPY MARRIAGE IS BASED ON MUTUAL TRUST - FOR INSTANCE, AT THIS VERY MOMENT MY WIFE THINKS I'M SLOGGING AT THE OFFICE.'

'WHEN IT CALMS DOWN, WE CAN GET IN SOME
PUTTING PRACTICE - WITHOUT A HOLE,
OF COURSE.'

'I SAID BRASSIE!'

'HERE THEY COME - NAPOLEON'S GLORIOUS ARMY TRUDGING BACK FROM MOSCOW . . .'

'I'M REALLY LOOKING FOR A SWING WHICH WILL
THRIVE ON NEGLECT.'

'NEVER MIND WHAT GARY PLAYER SAYS, YOUR
MOTHER SAYS EAT YOUR EGG.'

'I'M FED UP WITH ALL THIS TALK OF THE LARGER
AMERICAN BALL - WE WANT A LARGER HOLE!'

'WE'VE JUST HAD OUR FIRST QUARREL.'

'CAN YOU HONESTLY SAY THAT YOU LOVE ME
MORE THAN YOUR LITTLE FOUR-WOOD ?'

'IF YOU'LL PROMISE NOT TO SNEEZE WHEN I'M
DRIVING I'LL CUT OUT THE HICCUPPING AS
YOU PUTT.'

'NERO HAD HIS FIDDLE, DRAKE HIS BOWLS, I
HAVE MY GOLF . . . CLEAR ?'

'SLICING DOESN'T WORRY ME - NOW THAT I
KNOW IT'S A NATIONAL PROBLEM.'

'THERE ARE TWO QUESTIONS, AS I SEE IT, - ONE, WHAT CLUB WILL YOU USE ?, TWO, IS IT WORTH BREAKING YOUR NECK ? . . . '

'IT MAY HELP YOUR PUTTING CONCENTRATION,
BUT IT'S NOT DOING ANY GOOD TO THE
WALL-PAPER!'

'WE'VE EXTENDED THE STEWARD SERVICE -
REVIVAL PINTS AT THE EIGHTEENTH.'

'NEVER MIND WHAT HENRY COTTON SAID!'

'HEY! BEN HOGAN! - WHAT ABOUT TRYING A FEW
FULL-PIVOT SWINGS WITH THIS CARPET
BEATER . . .'

'IT'S NOT NICE BREAKING UP A FOUR-BALL.'

'ALL RIGHT, ALL RIGHT - THAT'S ENOUGH OF THE
SUBLIME ECSTASY . . .'

'YOU MUST BE WELL ROUND THE BEND TO DO
ANY GOOD AT THIS HOLE . . .'

'THE PRO NOW SAYS IT'S THE SWING THAT COUNTS - BEFORE, HE SAID THAT ALL I NEEDED WAS A NEW SET OF CLUBS!'

'I SEE YOU USING A NICE NEW SET OF WOODS,
DEEP-FACED, WITH WHIPPY SHAFTS . . .'

'MY THEORIES WILL STAND UP TO ANYTHING -
EXCEPT SHANKING.'

'YOU'RE RIGHT - IT'S A CHALLENGE!'

'ONCE UPON A TIME THERE WAS A WELSH
WIZARD - HIS NAME WAS DAI REES . . .'

'TOO WET FOR GOLF ? THAT'S A COWARDLY
THOUGHT - WAS IT TOO WET FOR WELLINGTON
TO WIN THE BATTLE OF WATERLOO ?'

'WILL YOU PLEASE THROW ANOTHER CLUB FOR
THE DAILY ECHO ?'

'SO YOU BROKE A HUNDRED! - WATCH ME SWELL
WITH PRIDE.'

'NOT A WORD DEAR, PLEASH-H, OR YOU'LL SPOIL
THE BESHT ROUND OF MY LIFE . . .'

'HERE'S A COURSE THAT SEPARATES THE MEN
FROM THE BOYS . . . !'

'APART FROM GOLF, HOW'S LIFE TREATING YOU ?'

'NOW THAT I CAN AFFORD TO BUY GOLF BALLS I
CAN'T HIT THEM FAR ENOUGH TO LOSE 'EM!'

'YOU DON'T OFTEN FIND A GREENSKEEPER AS
CONSCIENTIOUS AS OLD FRED.'

'SO YOU'RE BACK! - NO, DON'T TELL ME - I KNOW ..
THE PUTTS WOULDN'T DROP ... YOU SLICED OUT
OF BOUNDS AT THE THIRD ...'

'IF I GIVE YOU A BALL YOUR MA WILL SAY I'M
ENCOURAGING A BAD HABIT.'

'THE FIRST CAN BE REGARDED AS A PRACTICE
SWING!'

'AND TO THINK I COULD HAVE BEEN
PEACEFULLY LOSING MONEY AT CLUB HOUSE
BRIDGE!'

'FORE!'

'FOR TEN YEARS THE GOLF CLUB WAS MY
GREATEST JOY - THEN I BECAME A PLAYING
MEMBER . . .'

'AH WELL, WE ALL HAVE OUR SIMPLE
PLEASURES.'

'CHIPPING PRACTICE FOR ANOTHER HALF HOUR
- THEN DOWN WE GO FOR THE WORMS.'

'- AND THE MAIN THING IS TO BE RELAXED AND
ABSOLUTELY FREE . . .'